The Story of Bermondsey
by Mary Boast

London Borough of Southwark
Neighbourhood History No. 5

London Borough of Southwark
Southwark Local Studies Library

ISBN 0 905849 24 8
First published in 1978
Revised 1984
Reprinted with corrections 1998, 2003

© 1998 London Borough of Southwark

British Library Cataloguing in Publication Data

A catalogue record for this book is available from the British Library.
No part of this publication may be reproduced, stored in a retrieval system or transmitted by any means without prior permission of the Library and Information Services Manager.

Cover Illustrations

Front cover: Bermondsey Abbey's gateway and Bermondsey House, by C. Whichelo, 1805. St. Mary Magdalen's churchyard is in the foreground.
Inside front cover: The London and Greenwich Railway, c. 1836, showing the temporary station at Spa Road.
Inside back cover: St. Olave's Church, Tooley Street, 1811.

London Borough of Southwark Neighbourhood Histories

1. The Story of Camberwell
2. The Story of Dulwich
3. The Story of Peckham
4. The Story of Walworth
5. The Story of Bermondsey
6. The Story of Rotherhithe
7. The Story of The Borough
8. The Story of Bankside

NORTH
RIVER THAMES
HAYS DOCK
HMS Belfast
TOOLEY STREET
LONDON BRIDGE STATION
Pickle Herring
Potters Field
TOWER Bridge
Horsleydown Lane
Shad Thames
Queen Elizabeth St
ST SAVIOURS DOCK
Bermondsey Wall
Mill St
Jacob St
Wolseley St
Pier
DOCK HEAD
JAMAICA ROAD
Scott Lidgett Cres
Wilson Grove
Cherry Garden St
Keetons Rd
DRUMMOND ROAD
STORKS ROAD
ST JAMES'S ROAD
Thurland Rd
OLD JAMAICA ROAD
CLEMENTS RD
SPA ROAD
DRUID STREET
TANNER STREET
BERMONDSEY STREET
TOWER BRIDGE ROAD
RILEY ROAD
Crucifix La
Weston Street
Leathermarket St
Morocco St
LONG LANE
ABBEY STREET
Neckinger
The Grange
Grange Walk
GRANGE ROAD
TOWER BRIDGE RD
LEROY ST
Crimscott St
PAGES WALK
WILLOW WALK
OLD KENT ROAD
BRICKLAYERS ARMS GOODS STA.
DUNTON ROAD
SOUTHWARK PARK ROAD
Blue Anchor Lane
MONNOW RD
LYNTON ROAD
GALLEY WALL ROAD
VIADUCT
ROLLS ROAD
ROTHERHITHE NEW ROAD
SOUTH
2
3
4
5
6
7
8
9
10
12
13
14
15
16
17
18
19
20

Key to the map

1. Former Hay's Group Head Office; site of St. Olave's Church
2. Braidwood memorial
3. Lambeth College; formerly St. Olave's Grammar School
4. Statues of Colonel Bevington and Ernest Bevin
5. London City Mission; site of St. John's, Horselydown
6. Former Anchor Brewery of Courage & Co. Ltd.
7. Church of the Most Holy Trinity, Dockhead
8. Site of Jacob's Island
9. St. James's Church
10. Former biscuit factory of Peek, Frean & Co. Ltd.
11. Site of the first signal box
12. Blue Anchor Library
13. St. Anne's Church, Thorburn Square
14. Public Health Centre
15. Municipal offices; formerly the Town Hall
17. Bermondsey Square; site of Bermondsey Abbey
18. St. Mary Magdalen's Church
19. The Leather Market and Exchange
20. Southwark Crown Court

EAST

Based upon the Ordnance Survey mapping with permission of the Controller of Her Majesty's Stationery Office © Crown Copyright. Unauthorised reproduction infringes Crown Copyright and may lead to prosecution or civil proceedings. London Borough of Southwark LA086541/98/04.

Contents

	Introduction
1	Beornmund's Ey
3	Bermondsey Abbey
6	The Parish of St. Mary Magdalen
9	Bermondsey Spa and Other Entertainments
11	There's Nothing Like Leather
14	The First Railway in London
15	Crossing the Thames
17	Hay's Wharf and London's Larder
19	Food and Drink
21	Some Bermondsey Churches
22	Schools Past and Present
24	Hard Times
26	The Bermondsey Spirit
28	Dr. Salter and Other Pioneers
30	Bermondsey at War
31	Bermondsey Today
33	Bibliography
35	Index

The Story of Bermondsey

This booklet is a brief, simple introduction to the history of one part of the London Borough of Southwark. It is written mainly for young readers, whose home or school is in the former Metropolitan Borough of Bermondsey and covers this neighbourhood with the exception of Rotherhithe and the London Bridge area which are covered by other booklets in the series. Some suggestions for further reading are given at the end of the booklet. All the titles given are available at the Southwark Local Studies Library. Anyone wishing to make a more detailed study should visit this library at 211 Borough High Street, London, SE1 1JA (020 7403 3507). The library has a substantial collection of books, maps, illustrations, press-cuttings, microfilms and manuscripts covering all parts of the London Borough of Southwark. The opening hours may be obtained from any library. An appointment in advance is wise to use a microfilm reader or to consult manuscripts, and is essential in the case of school party visits.

Beornmund's Ey

Tower Bridge Road cuts through the middle of modern Bermondsey. Where this busy main road now crosses Abbey Street is the place where Bermondsey began well over a thousand years ago.

There is a green open space here, the old churchyard of St. Mary Magdalen Church. This is a good place to go if you want to try to imagine what Bermondsey was like in its early days. It was very quiet then. The land now covered by Bermondsey Square and the church was a low island rising slightly above the surrounding marshy ground. This was 'Beornmund's Ey', the island of Beornmund, probably an early Anglo-Saxon lord who owned the land. Birds such as gulls, ducks, heron, snipe, moorhens and kingfishers were to be seen and fish such as carp and salmon swam in the tidal streams. Bermondsey remained little changed for many years. According to a long poem by John Leland, published in 1545, 'Thou happy, snowy swan, hast thy serene abode, Where Barmsey (Bermondsey) of her well-known isles is proud'.

One of the streams was the Neckinger. You can follow its course from Grange Road, along Spa Road, along the road now called Neckinger, past the Neckinger Estate, along Abbey Street and George Row, to the east of St. Saviour's Dock, where it flowed out into the River Thames. The name, Willow Walk, reminds you of the willow trees that once overhung the stream. Galleywall is another old name: galley (or salley or sallow, as it was sometimes spelt) was an old word also meaning willow.

Much of Bermondsey is below the level of the River Thames at very high tides. A wall was built along the river bank to keep out the flood waters but often the water forced a hole in Bermondsey Wall and flooded the land. A breach in the wall at Rotherhithe is mentioned in the *Annals of Bermondsey Abbey* as early as 1230.

Walls became roads as people walked along the top of them to avoid the muddy ground. The road which runs by the river is still called Bermondsey Wall. Other walls or dykes divided and protected the land. Galley Wall was part of the boundary between Bermondsey, Rotherhithe and Camberwell.

The earliest description of Bermondsey is to be found in Domesday Book, the great survey of England compiled under William the Conqueror in 1086. Bermondsey was then a royal manor, belonging to King William. Domesday Book says there was some land for ploughing and growing corn, meadowland for cows and woods to provide nuts or acorns for pigs.

There was, however, one important building. According to Domesday Book, which was written in Latin, 'Ibi nova et pulchra ecclesia': 'there is a new and beautiful church'. For many centuries to come Bermondsey was known throughout England for the abbey built around this church.

Bermondsey Abbey

In the Middle Ages many people, wishing to devote their lives to the service of God, gave up all their worldly possessions and became monks living in monasteries. In those days Bermondsey had one of the greatest religious houses in the country.

Very long ago, about 700 A.D., there had been a small monastery here, founded by monks from the Abbey of St. Peter at Peterborough in Cambridgeshire. This completely disappeared. Perhaps, like Peterborough itself, it was destroyed during the Danish invasions. It was the new monastery, founded in 1082, which became the Bermondsey Abbey famous in history. Although this too has quite disappeared we know a good deal about it from old pictures, documents and finds by archaeologists, and it has left its mark for ever on the street map of Bermondsey.

Its founder was Aylwin Child, a citizen of London who, in 1082, gave the rents of some property in the City to the monastery of La Charité on the River Loire in France. In 1089 monks from La Charité, invited by Lanfranc, the Archbishop of Canterbury, came to start a monastery in Bermondsey. Its 'new and beautiful church' was dedicated to the Holy Saviour, or, as it is usually written, 'St. Saviour'.

La Charité came under an even more famous religious house, the Abbey of Cluny in eastern France. The monks of Bermondsey were Cluniac monks. They wore a black 'habit' or monk's dress, and like all Cluniacs obeyed a very strict rule. At first Bermondsey was known as a priory because it was under a prior who, himself, came under the Abbot of Cluny. In 1399 it became Bermondsey Abbey under an Englishman named John Attilburgh as Abbot.

About 1433, one of the monks wrote on parchment, in Latin, *The Annals of Bermondsey Abbey*. The book is now in the British Library. According to this, in 1117 the monks found, near the Thames, a holy cross, or rood. Soon pilgrims were coming from all over England to worship at the Rood of St. Saviour. After crossing Old London Bridge they would walk or ride down Bermondsey Street, a cross at Crucifix Lane marking the way. Long Lane was another old route to the abbey.

Kings, nobles and citizens gave rich gifts to Bermondsey Abbey and in time it came to own not only a great part of what is now the London Borough of Southwark but lands and churches throughout the length and breadth of England. It was a place of learning. The catalogue of its library, compiled in about 1310, is now in the Bodleian Library at Oxford.

Kings sometimes stayed at Bermondsey. Henry II spent Christmas in 1154 at the abbey. On 22nd April, 1250, an assembly of crusaders gathered there. At Bermondsey from 1202-1255 the king's justices held their courts, or 'eyres', for the County of Surrey. Two queens spent their last years at the abbey: Catherine de Valois, widow of Henry V, and Elizabeth Woodville, widow of Edward IV.

Bermondsey Abbey came to an end in 1538 when King Henry VIII dissolved the monasteries throughout England. Sir Thomas Pope bought the abbey church and demolished it. With the stones he built himself a fine mansion known as Bermondsey House.

Nothing now remains above ground of either Bermondsey Abbey or Bermondsey House but as you walk around Bermondsey streets, you can picture where they were. The main entrance to the abbey was through a gateway leading from Bermondsey Street into what is now Abbey Street (see the front cover). Bermondsey Square, where the antique market now attracts crowds on Friday mornings, was then the inner courtyard of the abbey. The abbey church, over 300 feet long, was on the line of Abbey Street, the altar being about where Abbey Street crosses Tower Bridge Road. Foundations of the church were excavated by archaeologists about forty years ago during the building of the St. Saviour's Estate.

Part of the stonework of the East Gate of the abbey is hidden behind the plaster wall of No. 7 Grange Walk. You can still see the two hinges of the gate on the outside of this house. Nos. 5-11 and also 67 Grange Walk are some of the oldest houses in Bermondsey, built three hundred years ago or more.

Many pieces of carved stone from the abbey have been found. Some are in the Cuming Museum, Walworth Road. The capital or top of a column is in St. Mary Magdalen's Church, and another is in Most Holy Trinity Church, Dockhead. St. Mary Magdalen's Church also owns one treasure which is said to have come from the abbey, a large silver dish, made about 1350. In the centre is a picture of a lady placing a helmet on a knight's head. The Bermondsey Dish is now in the Victoria and Albert Museum.

Old street names remind you of the abbey and also of other buildings of the time. Grange Road led to the abbey's grange or farm, at the corner of what is now called Spa Road. The abbey mill to grind the corn was turned by the millstream in Mill Street, not far from St. Saviour's Dock, where goods were landed for the Abbey of St. Saviour.

In the days of the abbey the riverside was lined with beautiful mansions which were the London residences of great men of the Church. The Abbot of Battle in Sussex had a house between Abbot's Lane and Battlebridge Lane. The bridge was over a stream which turned the abbot's watermill. Further down-river the Knights of St. John of Jerusalem also had watermills. Their street, 'St. John at Thames', has become Shad Thames. London Bridge Station now covers the site of the 'Inn', or town house, of the Prior of Lewes.

Tooley Street, one of the oldest streets in London, is a 'corruption' or mispronunciation of St. Olave's Street. For nearly nine hundred years there was a church here dedicated to St. Olave (or Olaf). St. Olaf House, near London Bridge, formerly the head office of the Hays Group, now stands on the site. Look out for the picture and story of St. Olave on the outside of the building. Look out also for the top of the tower of the church which has been set up in Tanner Street Recreation Ground.

Old houses in Grange Walk, one of which (behind the lamp) incorporates part of a mediaeval gateway of Bermondsey Abbey, including two hooks for the gate.

The Parish of St. Mary Magdalen

St. Mary Magdalen's Church, Bermondsey Street, 1852.

Bermondsey Street was the High Street of old Bermondsey. It is many hundreds of years older than Tower Bridge Road. As you walk up this narrow curving street, not a bit like a modern motorway, try to picture the scene when Bermondsey was just a village and all around were farms and market gardens which supplied produce for the City of London.

The most important building was, and still is, the Parish Church of St. Mary Magdalen, the oldest building in Bermondsey. It was built originally for the people who lived and worked on the abbey lands. In the church there is a list of rectors beginning with John de Ecclesia, John of the Church, who was rector in 1291. There have been many changes in the building since that date but part of the west wall and the lower part of the tower were built in the days of the abbey. Inside you can see the old stonework. In 1680 most of the church was rebuilt, much as it is today, except for the west front, which was rebuilt again in 1830.

The inside of the church is very light and beautiful. Behind the altar there is rich carving of the late 17th century. The wrought iron altar of the old St. Olave's Church has been placed in the south aisle as the two parishes of St. Mary Magdalen and St. Olave have now been united. The two large silver candelabra, or candleholders, were given to the church in 1698 and 1703.

Many thousands of babies have been christened in the church since records were first kept in 1548. The font which is now in use was set up in 1808. The parish registers with the names of all the people who have been christened, married or buried at the church are now in the London Metropolitan Archives. It is difficult to read many of the names on the old tombs in the churchyard but one is the tomb of the Rolls family who were big landowners and gave their name to Rolls Road.

A meeting of Bermondsey Borough Council in the session of 1902-3. Above the Mayor (Alexander Burton) are the borough's arms.

Before there was a Borough Council, the Parish of St. Mary Magdalen was governed by the Vestry, a committee of local people which met in the vestry of the church. The churchwardens were then not only concerned with the church, as they are today, but were important officials with many duties. They did their parish work in the Churchwardens' Pew which you can see at the back of the church. They probably used the desk to write up their accounts in their big leather-bound books. The account books of the Churchwardens and Overseers from 1599 are now in the Southwark Archives. The vestry minutes of the Parish of St. Olave, also in the archives, begin in 1552.

At the corner of Bermondsey Street and Abbey Street there is a curious small building which used to be the parish watchhouse. Before the days of the Metropolitan Police, it was the duty of the watchmen to keep law and order during the night. The Bermondsey watchmen reported at the watchhouse at 10.00 pm in summer and 9.00 pm in winter, each carrying a lantern with candle and a long staff, ready to set off on their rounds. According to their orders, if they found any 'malefactors, or disturbers of the King's Peace', they were to 'arrest and detain them in the watchhouse'.

Bermondsey Street has other very old buildings. The top floor of No. 78 juts out over the pavement. Many houses in Bermondsey must have looked like that at the time it was built, about 300 years ago.

Notice too the alleyways and courtyards leading off Bermondsey Street. Tyer's Gate and others are marked on Rocque's Map. Some were once entrances to inns and others to leatherworks. They still have an old type of road surface made of stone 'setts' or paving blocks, which were laid when the only traffic was horses and carts.

Bermondsey Spa and other entertainments

'Bittersweet grows by the ditchside against the garden wall of the Right Honourable the Earl of Sussex, his house in Bermondsey Street by London. And melons are in very great plenty'. This is how a famous book known as *Gerarde's Herbal* described Bermondsey in 1597. As you can see it was then a pleasant country village. Queen Elizabeth herself visited the Earl of Sussex who lived at the mansion built earlier by Sir Thomas Pope.

Near the river, where Tower Bridge Road is today, there were the meadows of Horselydown. In 1553 St. Olave's Vestry agreed that parishioners could keep their 'kyne' (cows) and horses on Horselydown, every owner paying 'for the going of every cow two pence a week and for every horse fourpence a week'. A painting of the time, which is now at Hatfield House, shows ladies and gentlemen dancing to the music of fiddlers at a wedding feast held out of doors on Horselydown.

No wonder people liked to come over to Bermondsey for a day's outing from the crowded City of London. They made their way across Old London Bridge or by ferry boat landing at one of the many riverside stairs. On 15th June 1664 Samuel Pepys recorded in his famous diary that he visited the Cherry Garden in what is now Cherry Garden Street and then returned 'singing finely' by boat to London Bridge. On the 14th April 1667, 'Lord's Day' (Sunday), he wrote, 'Took my wife and two of our maids over the water to Jamaica House – and there the girls did run for wagers over the bowling green'. Jamaica House was the famous tavern and gardens in Jamaica Road. It probably got its name soon after 1655, the year that Jamaica came under British rule.

In the 18th century well-to-do ladies and gentlemen believed it was good for their health to drink the water from a 'Spa' or spring containing some mineral salts. Bermondsey was in the fashion with its own Bermondsey Spa discovered in 1770 by Thomas Keyse in the grounds of his tea gardens in what is now Spa Road. He provided many kinds of entertainment for visitors. In addition to 'taking the waters' they could visit the picture gallery, of which he was very proud, as he was himself an artist, and the great Sir Joshua Reynolds, first President of the Royal Academy, had visited the gallery. In the evenings there were musical concerts and grand firework displays. Some of the songs written to be sung at Bermondsey Spa are now in Southwark Local Studies Library.

The William Curtis Ecological Park, which existed for a few years in recent times near the Bermondsey waterfront, would have pleased William Curtis, a neighbour of Thomas Keyse. In 1771 William Curtis, a famous botanist, set up on the site of Crimscott Street, the first scientific botanic garden for the study of British plants. Here he began publishing in 72 parts his *Flora Londinensis*.

Some of Bermondsey's old houses, such as Nos. 124-130 Jamaica Road, 8-11 Grange Road and 2-8 Bermondsey Square, were built about the time of Thomas Keyse and William Curtis and their first residents may well have enjoyed the delights of Bermondsey Spa.

Soon, however, Bermondsey began to change. In 1779 Curtis moved to Lambeth. Bermondsey Spa closed in 1804. Even in early times Bermondsey had always had some famous industries. Now it became one of the main centres of trade and industry in the London area and all its pleasure-gardens, market gardens and farms were built over with crowded streets.

There's nothing like leather

Boots and shoes, saddles and reins, gloves and bags: these are just a few of the things which are made from leather. In the days when everyone travelled on foot, on horseback, or by horsedrawn vehicles, and long before plastic was in use, no wonder people said 'there's nothing like leather'. And ever since the Middle Ages the chief place in England for the manufacture of leather was Bermondsey.

Bermondsey had four things needed for this industry. Firstly, it could get a good supply of animal skins to make into leather from the butchers of London. In fact, in 1392, a proclamation ordered that the butchers should have a place in Southwark for dumping such 'garbage'. Leather-making was actually just one of the unpleasant, smelly, smoky or dangerous trades which the citizens were glad not to have within the City walls but across the river in Southwark and Bermondsey. Secondly, the process of tanning, that is, preserving the skins and transforming them into leather, includes washing and long soaking in tan-pits. Bermondsey had a good supply of water for this process in its many streams and ditches which rose and fell every twelve hours with the tide in the River Thames. Tanners' yards are marked on Rocque's Map all along Long Lane and by the Grange. Thirdly, oak-bark was much used in tanning. In early times there were woods in Bermondsey where oaks may have grown and also not far away, as you can tell from place-names such as Forest Hill and Honor Oak. Fourthly, the Bermondsey workers could be sure of a good market for their leather to the citizens of London, just across Old London Bridge.

Leather work at all stages from tanning to the finished product needs skilled craftsmen. This and other industries in Bermondsey were helped by expert immigrant workers who came and settled along the Bermondsey riverside. Many of these were 'Flemings', that is, they came from Flanders, the modern Belgium and Holland. In fact, so many were living here that there was a special Flemish Burial Ground where London Bridge Station is today. Later came the Huguenots, or French Protestants, who escaped to England, especially after 1685 because they were no longer allowed freedom of worship in their own country.

The staff of the leather manufacturing firm of George Whichelow, c.1900.

If you walk around Bermondsey you are continually reminded of the leather industry. Leading off Bermondsey Street there are Tanner Street and Morocco Street, which is named after a kind of leather made from goatskins. Leathermarket Street leads to the Leather Exchange, a fine building erected in 1879. Notice the plaques on it showing various processes of the leather industry.

Even public houses have names from the leather trade, for example, *Simon the Tanner* in Long Lane. Nos. 146-148 Long Lane, built about 1730, were once the home of well-to-do leather merchants. They have carved marble mantlepieces with scenes of the leather trade. In the days when your parents or grandparents were young you would also have smelt the strong smell of tanning. Bermondsey's famous old leather firms now do their tanning elsewhere.

One of the oldest and most important firms was Bevingtons', which only moved out about 1981. Their impressive building is still standing in Abbey Street. Three brothers, Samuel, Henry and Timothy Bevington, started leather manufacturing in Bermondsey in 1800. They made good use of the Neckinger stream which flowed through

Lime pits at the Neckinger Leather Mills of Bevingtons and Sons, 1931.

their works. The grandson of one of the founders, Samuel Bourne Bevington, was Colonel of the local Volunteer Regiment and the first Mayor of Bermondsey in 1900. You can see his statue in Queen Elizabeth Street, near Tower Bridge.

Other industries grew up using the waste materials from leatherwork, for example, Bermondsey was noted for its hatters who used the wool removed from sheepskins. Christy's of Bermondsey Street, at one time the largest manufacturer of hats in the world, moved out only in 1972. The sign of a Woolpack once named a pub in Bermondsey Street.

Over an archway in Grange Road there are the words Alaska factory, a figure of a seal and the date of 1869. This was the entrance to Martin's, the fur merchants. When the firm started, sealskin jackets were in fashion and seals were hunted off the coast of Alaska.

The National Leathersellers' College was in Tower Bridge Road but moved to Northampton in 1977.

The First Railway in London

If you look up from almost any street in Bermondsey you see railway arches. This wonderful viaduct of 878 brick arches was built in 1834 to carry London's first passenger railway over open country from London to Greenwich. The first part to be completed was from Spa Road to Deptford. The Spa Road Station was the first railway terminus in London. The first train, with an engine like Stephenson's *Rocket,* ran on 8th February 1836. On the 14th December the Lord Mayor of London rode on the first train out of London Bridge Station. Soon there were trains every quarter of an hour from 8 am to 10 pm and fares were advertised as 'Imperial carriages one shilling, open cars sixpence'.

In those early days there was no British Rail. Many companies were constructing railways. Next after the London and Greenwich came the London and Croydon in 1839. The two lines joined at Corbett's

Spa Road Station, c.1910. The station was closed in 1915 but the entrance remains.

Lane so here, to prevent two trains crashing, the first signal box in the world was erected. White and red lights were used at night and the signal-box was sometimes known as 'the lighthouse'. The London Brighton and South Coast Railway was opened in 1841 and the South Eastern or Dover Railway in 1842. If you go by train to London Bridge you can see how wide the tracks are to carry all these and other lines. From South Bermondsey Station you get an exciting view of the viaducts.

In the past few years London Bridge Station has been almost completely rebuilt. Today well over 50 million passengers travel into or out of it every year.

Spa Road Station closed in 1915 but you can still read the words 'Booking Office' under the arches in Priter Way. The entrance to the old station was restored in 1986. Another old station, the Bricklayers' Arms, in Old Kent Road, closed in 1980. It was originally built for passengers but later was used only for goods' trains.

Crossing the Thames

One of the sights of London that every tourist knows is Tower Bridge. You can hardly imagine Bermondsey without the bridge, or Tower Bridge Road, but both were built only 100 years ago.

Until 1894 there was no bridge lower down river than London Bridge. In earlier times people who wanted to cross the river east of London Bridge went by ferry boat. Many little old streets in Bermondsey led to steps going down to the river, for example, Battlebridge Stairs, Pickle Herring Stairs, Horselydown Stairs, Cherry Garden Stairs.

In 1869 the Tower Subway was constructed. This was an iron tube seven feet wide, which ran under the river from Vine Lane, Tooley Street to Tower Hill. One entrance may still be seen. Twelve people at a time could travel in a little carriage which was drawn through the subway by a steel cable. Later this was removed and people were allowed to walk across, paying a halfpenny a time. Before Tower Bridge was built about a million people used the subway every year.

Tower Bridge was opened on 30th June, 1894. Because it led to the Tower of London the architect, J. Wolfe Barry, copied the style of architecture of the Middle Ages. Tower Bridge, however, had to go up and down, regularly, without delay, to allow ships to go through to unload at the wharves along the river bank. The engineer, Horace Jones, therefore, had to provide the bridge with most efficient machinery. Hydraulic power, that is water pressure, was used to raise the bridge.

On the east side near the former Courage's Brewery, you can see the chimney of the boilerhouse. Steam engines were used to raise the pressure of the water. On the west side of the bridge are the workshops which kept the machinery in good order. In the Tower Bridge Museum below Tower Bridge Road you can see the original boilers and engines and an exhibition explaining how they worked and by the south tower of the bridge you can view one of the control cabins.

Today fewer boats come up the river so Tower Bridge goes up and down less often. When it does so it is raised by electricity. The upper walkways were reopened in 1982.

Hay's Wharf and London's Larder

Until a few years ago the whole Bermondsey waterfront down to Tower Bridge, and similarly along Shad Thames, around St. Saviour's Dock and along Bermondsey Wall, was lined with warehouses built right to the water's edge. This was then a very busy area. There were always ships alongside the warehouses and cranes jutting out over the river landing goods brought from all over the world. Large ocean-going vessels which came up river only as far as the Surrey Docks transferred their cargoes to lighters, or smaller ships, for landing at the Bermondsey warehouses.

This stretch of the river was known as 'London's larder' or 'the breakfast-table of London', as three-quarters of the butter, cheese and canned meat needed for London was stored there. Many Bermondsey men were employed in this vital work of handling London's food.

One company owned very many of the warehouses, the famous Hay's Wharf Company. Its founder was Alexander Hay who, in 1651, took over some property near the small inlet of the Thames later known as Hay's Dock. Over the years Hay's Wharf became more and more prosperous, taking over wharves and warehouses all along the riverfront as far as Tower Bridge.

Shad Thames, 1971. Wharves on both sides of the road are connected by metal bridges at various heights.

The one danger which always threatened Hay's Wharf was fire, especially in the past when the warehouses were stacked with inflammable goods such as tallow for making candles. The worst occasion was the Great Tooley Street fire of June, 1861, which raged for two weeks. For Londoners it was the sight of their lives.

But the damage to property was said to be over £2,000,000 and the brave Superintendent of the London Fire Engine Establishment, James Braidwood, was killed when a warehouse exploded. There is a memorial to him high up on the wall of 33 Tooley Street. Carved in stone are his fireman's helmet and axe. One result of the fire was the setting up of the Metropolitan or London Fire Brigade.

In spite of this set-back Hay's Wharf continued to prosper. The warehouses around Hay's Dock, built about 1856, were restored and beautiful clipper ships, rather like the Cutty Sark, which you can see at Greenwich, used to land there with the new season's tea from China.

Later, steamers replaced sailing ships. Look out for the stone model of one, high up on the outside of 15 Tooley Street. Next door is a building formerly called Colonial House (now part of London Bridge Hospital). With faster, refrigerated ships, butter and cheese could be brought all the way from Australia and New Zealand, which, when Colonial House was built, were colonies of the British Empire. Hay's Wharf Company were very go-ahead in installing cold storage in their warehouses to store these perishable foods.

Tea chests at Hay's Wharf, c.1920.

About 1970 a great period of Bermondsey and London history came to an end. The Surrey Docks at Rotherhithe and other London docks were closed. Goods are now brought from overseas by large container ships which need more space and deeper water so they dock nearer the mouth of the Thames at Tilbury. There are few ships on the river, apart from HMS Belfast, the World War II cruiser brought here in 1971 as a tourist attraction.

Most of the warehouses were no longer needed for their original purpose. Many have been demolished leaving large open spaces, particularly near Tower Bridge. Others have been restored and converted, some even into luxury flats.

New developments have taken the place of the old warehouses. A large development called London Bridge City was completed in the late 1980s between London Bridge and Battlebridge Lane, comprising a mixture of completely new buildings and restored wharfs. The old Hay's Dock was filled in and roofed over, and now serves as Hay's Galleria, consisting of shops and offices. Battlebridge Lane also leads to Southwark Crown Court, opened in 1983.

Food and Drink

When you think of food and drink you usually think of certain 'household names'. Many of these famous firms started in Bermondsey. Peek Frean's biscuits and Sarson's vinegar were among the last to leave. Courage's beer moved out only in 1981.

Even in the Middle Ages, brewing was an important Bermondsey industry. Brewers did good business selling their ale to the travellers who passed through the neighbourhood on their way to and from the City. The 'Flemings' and Germans who settled along the riverside brought their skills to the trade. They started adding hops to give the beer its typical bitter taste and to make it keep longer and Borough High Street and parts of Bermondsey became a centre for hop merchants. Courage's was founded in 1787 by John Courage, who came from Scotland. The business grew and grew and took over many other firms including Barclay Perkins, another very old brewery in Park Street, Southwark. You can see the former Courage's Anchor Brewery from Tower Bridge or from Horselydown Lane.

The strong scent of brewing was one of the well-known Bermondsey smells. On the other side of Tower Bridge Road there was a different scent. This came from Sarson's vinegar brewery. There was a vinegar yard on the site of Sarson's from at least 1812.

As foodstuffs from all over the world were landed and stored at Bermondsey it was only natural that here there were many processing and packaging firms. Pearce Duff's made custard powder at their factory in Spa Road, Crosse and Blackwell's made pickles in Crimscott Street and Hartley's jams were in Tower Bridge Road. Jacob's biscuits were in Wolseley Street, Dockhead. All these firms have now moved out of Bermondsey. Peek Frean's in Drummond Road, which stayed rather longer, was founded in 1857 by Mr. Peek, a City tea merchant, who provided the money, and Mr. Frean, his niece's husband, a ship's biscuit-maker, who provided the 'know-how'. Before their time, manufactured biscuits were as hard as bricks and not very tasty. John Carr, a friend of George Frean, who soon joined the firm, started making the light, crispy, crumbly biscuits we like today, and soon people were buying Peek Frean's biscuits all over the world. Until 1983 Spiller's dog biscuits were also made in Bermondsey. The firm was in Jacob Street for nearly 80 years.

Bermondsey was the place where tinned food began. These days you can hardly imagine a kitchen cupboard not stocked with tins or cans. Before fridges and freezers were invented, tins were even more important. In 1811, an engineer named Bryan Donkin, who had a factory in Grange Road, introduced into England the first process ever used here for tinning meat. Two years later he sent some samples of his tinned beef to Kensington Palace and received a letter of thanks saying 'your patent beef was tasted by the Queen, the Prince Regent and several distinguished personages and highly approved'. In 1824 Donkin's tins of soup were taken on an Arctic expedition. When some of the tins were opened in 1937, 113 years later, the soup was still edible. In 1902 Bryan Donkin's company moved to Chesterfield. Another famous firm in Bermondsey was the Metal Box Company, which made tins in Riley Road until it moved out in 1982.

When Bermondsey's trade and industry was at its height, road transport was horsedrawn. At 217 Long Lane there used to be a stable block on three floors that was once a 'multi-storey horse park'.

Some Bermondsey Churches

From many parts of Bermondsey you can see, standing out above the roof tops, the clock tower of St. James's Church, near Jamaica Road. Apart from St. Mary Magdalen's, this is the oldest church still in use in Bermondsey. It was built in 1829, when the population of Bermondsey was just beginning to increase and could seat nearly 2,000 people. With its great columns at the entrance it looks rather like an ancient Greek temple. Look out for other London churches in this style. Sometimes they are known as 'Waterloo churches' because they were built with money granted by Parliament after the Battle of Waterloo. The bells of St. James's were cast from cannon captured at Waterloo.

The Roman Catholic Church of the Most Holy Trinity, Dockhead, is a more modern building, consecrated in 1960. It replaces an older church which was destroyed in the war. The architect, H.S. Goodhart-Rendel, said the design was based on an equilateral triangle to represent the Holy Trinity. The Catholics of Bermondsey are proud of their history. In the church there is a chapel dedicated to the Blessed John and Thomas Felton who were both martyred for their faith in the 16th century. When he was arrested, John Felton was living in part of the old Bermondsey Abbey buildings, and his son, Thomas, was born there. Many Bermondsey Catholic families came later from Ireland, to work in the tanneries, docks and railways and then settled and made their home here. The Convent of Mercy, Dockhead, was founded in 1839 by an Irish nun, Catherine McAuley. Sisters from the convent went to help Florence Nightingale in the Crimean War.

During the reign of Queen Victoria, as the population increased, many more churches and chapels were built, for example, Our Lady of La Salette, Melior Street, 1861, Drummond Road Baptist Church in 1866, St. Anne's, Thorburn Square in 1869, St. Bartholomew's, Barkworth Road, 1877, St. Augustine's, Lynton Road, 1882, and the South London (Methodist) Mission, Bermondsey Street, in 1900. The Bermondsey Gospel Mission in Old Jamaica Road was begun in 1864 by Walter Ryall, who had been a deep-sea fisherman and set up a mission for the people of Dockhead and a school for very poor children. Everyone loved the beautiful voice of his daughter, Annie

Ryall, who grew up to become a celebrated singer. After her father's death she and her husband, William Bustin, carried on the mission. From 1919-22 William Bustin was Mayor of Bermondsey. The Gedling Mission started in 1881. For over 60 years much good work was done here by Alexander Brown and his family.

Two of Bermondsey's oldest churches are now no more. By 1928 the railway and warehouses had taken over most of St. Olave's parish so the church was demolished. St. John's, Horselydown, built in 1732, was destroyed in the war. People nicknamed this church 'lousy St. John's'. The weather vane on its spire, which was actually a comet, looked from a distance like a small insect. The vane is now inside the London City Mission, 175 Tower Bridge Road, which has been built on the site.

Schools Past and Present

In Tooley Street near Tower Bridge there is a large Victorian building now occupied by Lambeth College, but built for St. Olave's Grammar School, the oldest school in Bermondsey, founded in 1561. The first school was near St. Olave's Church but, with the coming of the railway, it moved to the other end of Tooley Street. For 400 years, Bermondsey boys attended this school. Like all educated gentlemen in the past they were especially well taught in the classical languages, Latin and Greek. In 1968 St. Olave's moved out to Orpington.

Other schools were started by people who wanted to give even the poorest children a chance of learning to read and write. There are boards in St. Mary Magdalen's Church recording some of their names. Until 1830 there was a girls' school in a room over the church porch. The building in Grange Walk to which it moved still has the inscription 'Bermondsey United Charity School for Girls, erected AD 1830'. Charities provided centuries ago by people from all the old parishes, St. Mary Magdalen, St. Olave, St. John and St. Thomas, have been put together and the Charities Office in Druid Street still makes good use of the money to help both schoolchildren and old people.

Bacon's is the oldest school still in Bermondsey. It was founded in 1718 with money left by Josiah Bacon. It used to be in Grange Road, but has moved to Timber Pond Road in the Surrey Docks. At first the school was intended for 40-60 boys. Now nearly 1,000 boys and girls are educated at Bacon's. The Boutcher School, Grange Road, was founded in 1871 by William Boutcher, in memory of his wife.

Schools for Catholic children were started by Holy Trinity Church in 1800. They have grown to become St. Joseph's School, George Row, and St. Michael's, John Felton Road.

Handicapped children were not forgotten in Bermondsey. The first school in England for the deaf and dumb was started in Grange Road in 1792. The founders were the Reverend Henry Cox Mason, curate and afterwards Rector of St. Mary Magdalen's, and John Townsend, minister of a chapel in Jamaica Row. There is a memorial in St. Mary Magdalen's to the first teacher, Joseph Watson. The school later moved to Old Kent Road where it remained until the building of the flyover forced it to move out to Tulse Hill.

In 1870 an important Education Act set up 'School Boards', or committees, to provide enough places for all children to go to school. So, in the next few years, many 'Board Schools' were built. Some are still in use today, for example, Snowsfields, which has on the outside the letters LSB and the date it was enlarged, 1900.

Hard Times

17,169 people lived in the Parish of St. Mary Magdalen, Bermondsey, in 1801. By 1881 its population was 86,652. The population of London and the whole of England increased enormously during this period. In Bermondsey, where trade and industry flourished, people came from other parts to seek work in the docks, railways and factories.

Southwark Park Road, c.1928. This was Bermondsey's high street.

Where, and how did they all live? For those in steady jobs or a little better off there were pleasant Victorian houses of a type which people appreciate today, as in the streets between Lynton Road and Southwark Park Road. But for the thousands of very poor people in Bermondsey, row upon row of narrow streets and alleys were hastily put up, completely covering what had once been open fields. Families shared crowded little houses, built back to back, as close as possible. Sometimes as many as nine people lived in one room. Often there was no water supply, only a tap in the street to serve up to twenty-five houses, and there was no proper sanitation.

For the poorest of all, the old, the orphans, the unemployed, there was the workhouse in Tanner Street. If you have read Oliver Twist you will have some idea of what life was like in a workhouse. In the same novel, written in 1838, Charles Dickens also described Bermondsey's worst area, 'Jacob's Island', the place where according to the story, Bill Sikes finally met his end. It was between what is now Jacob Street and the river and at high tide was actually an island, cut off by the mill stream or 'Folly Ditch'. Old tumbledown houses overlooked the ditch from which the unfortunate inhabitants had to draw up all the water they needed in buckets, and the same ditch served as a sewer. No wonder terrible diseases, such as cholera, broke out in such a neighbourhood. About 1860, these horrible ditches were filled in and the old houses were demolished.

Large blocks of flats or 'tenements' began to be built for some working people, for example, Devon Mansions, Tooley Street, erected in 1875, and the Guinness Trust Buildings in Snowsfields, which have on the outside the date 1897, the year of Queen Victoria's Diamond Jubilee. But many old slums, and the bad unhealthy conditions, remained. People still worked long hours for low pay, or were unemployed, as dock work was very uncertain. They lacked nourishing food and suffered particularly from tuberculosis, from which many died each year.

Churches and Christian missions did what they could to help, for example, the South London Mission provided free breakfasts for large numbers of hungry schoolchildren. The Gedling Street Mission had a soup kitchen. A great deal of good was done by people from Oxford and Cambridge Universities who came to live and work in Bermondsey. They concentrated especially on providing free medical treatment for poor people who could not afford doctors' fees. Dr. John Stansfeld, with the help of students from Oxford, founded the Oxford Medical Mission and in 1906, students from Cambridge founded the Cambridge University Medical Mission. Young people still enjoy the clubs and other activities started by both missions. The Bermondsey Medical Mission for Women in Grange Road, was started in 1904 by a wonderful woman, Dr. Selina Fox.

The Reverend John Scott Lidgett of the Methodist Church saw that the people of Bermondsey had another need. Boys and girls left their 'Board' or 'Elementary' school at fourteen and there was no chance for them or older people to continue their education. People were hungry for learning and for music, art and theatre. The Bermondsey Settlement which he opened in 1892 in Farncombe Street had a lecture room, a gymnasium and a library. Concerts and art exhibitions were presented and all kinds of exciting activities. There was a dramatic society and a football club and visits to interesting places. For the younger children there was a Guild of Play. The Settlement closed in 1967.

The Bermondsey Spirit

A women's outing or 'beano', photographed in front of the Old Margate Town, George Row, c.1930.

It was during these hard times that something special developed in Bermondsey, what might be called 'the Bermondsey spirit'. Bermondsey (excluding Rotherhithe) is a small place, only about one mile from east to west and one mile north to south. People lived close together in their little streets and courtyards and worked together in factories, wharves and docks near their homes. Families stayed together. They knew their neighbours, who were mostly poor, like themselves. It was a real community. People shared their joys and sorrows and helped each other in time of trouble. Hard times did not seem so hard because of this 'togetherness', and despite hardships, older people in Bermondsey often look back on 'the good old days', for they also found plenty in life to enjoy together. For example, they remember the friendly, lively crowds 'down the Blue', the market in Blue

The Star Cinema, Abbey Street, 1937, showing the 'tuppenny rush'.

Anchor Road, or, as it is now called, Southwark Park Road, where they went late on Saturday nights to spend their hard-earned wages. Before modern traffic took over there were over two hundred stalls lining each side of the road. Now, all that remains of this old street market are the stalls in Market Place.

A real treat was a visit to the Star in Abbey Street. In the days of Queen Victoria this was a music hall. Later it became a cinema, known as 'the la de da', or 'the tuppenny rush' as the cheapest seats were only two old pence. Other popular cinemas included the Stork in Stork's Road, the Trocette in Tower Bridge Road, the Grand, Grange Road, the Rialto, St. James's Road, and the Palace, Southwark Park Road.

Dr. Salter and other pioneers

Alfred Salter, the most important man in Bermondsey's recent history, first got to know conditions here when he was studying medicine at Guy's Hospital. He was a brilliant student, winning three gold medals, but decided to devote his life to Bermondsey. He was a Quaker, a member of the Religious Society of Friends. In 1898 he joined the Bermondsey Settlement, where Ada, the lady who became his wife, was also working. In 1900 he set up as a doctor in Jamaica Road. Charging his poor patients only sixpence a visit, or treating them free of charge, he gave them so much care and courtesy that women said, 'he treats you as though you were a duchess', and everyone loved 'the doctor on the bike'.

Both Alfred and Ada knew, however, that the only real cure for Bermondsey's ills was to improve living conditions for the people and to do this they must take part in local government and politics. In 1900 the old parishes of St. Mary Magdalen, St. Olave and St. John, with St. Thomas and St. Mary, Rotherhithe, had joined together to form the Metropolitan Borough of Bermondsey. In 1903 Alfred Salter was elected to the Borough Council. In 1922 he became Bermondsey's first Labour Member of Parliament. When Ada joined the Bermondsey Council in 1910 she was the first woman councillor in London. In 1922 she became Mayor of Bermondsey.

Neckinger Estate, 1938: a block of Bermondsey Borough Council's flats when new.

The Salters and others on the Council had very far-sighted ideas. In place of overcrowded streets they wanted to make Bermondsey into a 'garden city'. Salisbury Street, near the river, was one of the worst areas. Dr. Salter described it as 'a death trap and fever den'. It was rebuilt and renamed Wilson Grove. Now it looks like a pleasant village street and has been designated the 'Alfred Salter Conservation Area'. Unfortunately there was not enough money to rebuild all Bermondsey in this way, but, wherever possible, bad housing and slums were demolished. Generally they were replaced by blocks of flats. A good example is the Neckinger Estate built in 1938.

In the old houses, with no bathrooms and often no running water, it was difficult to keep clean. There were no launderettes in those days. In 1927, therefore, the Council built a magnificent 'palace of baths', with baths, public laundry and swimming bath. In the early years people queued to use them. After nearly fifty years the Grange Road Baths were demolished because of structural weakness.

Another important building of those days, the Public Health Centre in Grange Road, is still used for various health purposes. More than twenty years before there was a National Health Service, Dr. Salter set up here a Health Service for Bermondsey. Before modern drugs were discovered, sunshine was the only cure for tuberculosis, the disease which afflicted so many poor people, especially children. At the Centre there was a 'Solarium', where lamps provided 'artificial sunshine'.

All kinds of good things were happening in Bermondsey in those years. A Beautification Committee planted trees in the streets and flowers in every open space, such as the old churchyards of St. Mary Magdalen and St. James. Ordinary people had flowers in their window-boxes. For the children, swings were put in the Long Lane Playground and in St. James's churchyard there was the first covered slide in England, given by Arthur Carr of Peek, Frean's. The Tanner Street Recreation Ground, on the site of the old workhouse, was opened in 1929. At the Central Library, Spa Road, built in 1892, there were exhibitions and lectures, and concerts took place next door in the Town Hall.

Dr. Alfred Salter plants a tree during the opening of Tanner Street Recreation Ground in May, 1929. Councillor George Horwood, the Mayor of Bermondsey, stands on the right.

In the 1920s and 1930s Bermondsey was transformed and people came from far away to get ideas on housing, health and beautification from Bermondsey.

Bermondsey at War

Bermondsey suffered and showed great courage in both World Wars. The names of 1,274 men are inscribed in the Bermondsey and Rotherhithe Roll of Honour of those who were killed or died of wounds in what was then known as the Great War, 1914-18. Go and look at the Bermondsey and Rotherhithe War Memorial in West Lane and a memorial to the men of the Queen's, Bermondsey's Regiment, in Old Jamaica Road. One of the Bermondsey heroes was Corporal Frederick Holmes, who won the Victoria Cross. In France, under enemy gunfire, he carried a wounded comrade about three miles to safety and then went back to rescue a gun carriage and prevent it falling into enemy hands.

In World War II Bermondsey itself, with its docks, warehouses, factories and railways, and on the route to central London, was right in the front line. Bombs fell here more often and more continuously than in almost any place in the British Isles. People spent night after night in shelters but even here they were not always safe. A bomb killed sixty-three people sheltering under the Stainer Street railway arch near London Bridge Station. On May 11th, 1941, a bomb fell on the Town Hall, killing the Mayor, Councillor Henley, who was fighting incendiary bombs. Among the heroes of this war were Joe Blake, Chief Staff Officer of the Civil Defence, who was awarded the George Medal, and Albert Heming, who won the George Cross. For three hours, Heming dug upside down through rubble to rescue a man in a house which had been struck by a V2 rocket. It took him another hour to drag the man back to safety through the tunnel he had made. At least 709 civilians were killed in the war and thousands were injured. More than three thousand homes were destroyed and nearly all were damaged. Bermondsey men and women played their part also in all the armed services. The Victoria Cross was awarded to Lieutenant Alec Horwood, son of a Mayor of Bermondsey, who died leading an attack in Burma.

Bermondsey Today

There have been many changes in Bermondsey during the past thirty years. Firstly, it looks very different from the Bermondsey your grandparents knew as children. After the war an enormous amount of rebuilding had to be done both because of the destruction by bombing and also to complete the programme of slum clearance. In the 1960s and 1970s large areas were completely redeveloped.

Secondly, in 1965, by Act of Parliament, Bermondsey was joined with the Metropolitan Boroughs of Camberwell and Southwark to form the London Borough of Southwark. The people of Bermondsey no longer had a separate Borough Council but elected members to represent them on the Southwark Borough Council.

Thirdly, the Surrey Docks at Rotherhithe were closed in 1970 and with them many of the Bermondsey warehouses. A whole way of life has changed and it has been a sad time for men who had always worked by the river. Many industries have also closed, or moved out of London. Yet, in spite of all the changes, if you walk round Bermondsey you always see something to remind you of its history. For example, go down the steps on the east side of Tower Bridge Road and explore one of Bermondsey's conservation areas. Walk past Horselydown Lane and along Shad Thames which looks almost like a secret passage as it curves round St. Saviour's Dock. Overhead are walkways which were used to transfer goods landed at the dock to warehouses on the other side of the street. The scent of spices lingered about them until recently. After mounting the steps for a good view of the dock itself at Dockhead, make your way along Mill Street and past Jacob Street to Bermondsey Wall, all names and places which will have a meaning for you.

Even your nearest playground can be a place of interest and worth treating with care. The Tooley Street playground was a burial ground for St. Olave's parish from 1586 until 1853. A few of the old tombstones are still there to tell of families who lived in the parish long ago. The playground in Long Lane was a Quaker burial ground.

Archaeologists found pottery made over 350 years ago near the little street still called Potters' Fields. A Blue Anchor Tavern in what is now Southwark Park Road, is marked on a map of 1696. The inscription 'Fort Place' on the side wall of the Grange pub is a reminder of the fort erected near here by Parliament during the Civil War. Names of modern housing estates and schools are usually chosen as reminders of Bermondsey history, for example, the Dickens Estate near 'Jacob's Island'.

People are right to be proud to say, 'I am from Bermondsey'. This little area has a great history. In the Middle Ages there was its abbey. In Victorian times it was at the centre of London's trade and industry. Later it took a lead in social reform. Now is a time of change when Bermondsey, like its neighbours in North Southwark and Rotherhithe, awaits new developments. The 'Bermondsey Spirit' which has survived hard times and good times is needed now, and not only in Bermondsey. With it you can begin to plan for Bermondsey's and Southwark's future.

Select Bibliography

Edward T Clarke, *Bermondsey / Its Historic Memories and Associations* (1901).

G.W. Phillips, *The History and Antiquities of the Parish of Bermondsey* (1841).

V. Leff and C.H Blunden, *Riverside Story/The Story of Bermondsey and its People* (1965).

Victoria County History of Surrey, Vol. IV, pp. 17-24 (1912).

W. Lees Bell, *The History of Bermondsey* (1880).

Rose Graham, *The Priory of La Charité-sur-Loire and the Monastery of Bermondsey* (1926).

A.R. Martin, *On the Topography of the Cluniac Abbey of St. Saviour at Bermondsey* (1926).

Geoffrey T. Gray, *The Parish Church of St. Mary Magdalen Bermondsey* (1958).

George Dodd, *Days at the Factories* (1843). This book gives accounts of Christy's hat factory and Bevingtons' tannery.

Geoffrey Bevington, *Bevingtons and Sons/Bermondsey/1795-1950* (1993).

Arthur Sadler, *One Hundred and Seventy Five Years of the House of Christy* (1949).

R.H.G. Thomas, *London's First Railway/The London and Greenwich* (1972).

O.S. Nock, *The South Eastern and Chatham Railway* (1961).

Theo Crosby, *The Necessary Monument* (1970). This book is an account of Tower Bridge.

Aytoun Ellis, *Three Hundred Years on London River* (1952). A thorough history of Hay's Wharf and its associated businesses.

Sally Holloway, *London's Noble Fire Brigades 1833-1904* (1973). The great fire of Tooley Street in 1861 and James Braidwood's death in it are recounted in this work.

Courage & Co. Ltd., Anchor Brewhouse, Horselydown, 150th Anniversary, 1787-1937.

Peek, Frean & Co. Ltd., *1857-1957/A Hundred Years of Biscuit Making.*

Bridget Cherry and Nikolaus Pevsner, *The Buildings of England / London 2; South* (1983).

Ruth Kendall, *History of St. James Church Bermondsey* (1979).

L.J. Bourdelot, *The Story of the Catholic Church in Bermondsey* (1923).

L.E. Whatmore, *The Story of Dockhead Parish* (1960).

Harvest of Mercy/Bicentenary of the Birth of Catherine McAuley 1778-1978. This pamphlet and the next one concern the history of the Convent of Mercy at Dockhead.

Letters from Florence Nightingale to Reverend Mother Clare Moore (1982).

John D. Beasley, *The Bitter Cry Heard and Heeded/The Story of the South London Mission 1889-1989* (1989).

Cast Your Net/The Centenary History of the Bermondsey Gospel Mission (1964).

R.C. Carrington, *Two Schools/A History of St. Olave's and St. Saviour's Grammar School Foundation* (1971).

Barclay Baron, *The Doctor/The Story of John Stansfeld of Oxford and Bermondsey* (1952).

J. Scott Lidgett, *The Aims and Work of the Bermondsey Settlement* (1891).

J. Scott Lidgett, *My Guided Life* (1936).

D.M. Connan, *A History of the Public Health Department in Bermondsey* (1935).

David Dunn, *A Bermondsey Boy Remembers* (1992).

Fenner Brockway, *Bermondsey Story/The Life of Alfred Salter* (1949).

Twelve Years of Labour Rule on the Bermondsey Borough Council 1922-1934.

J.D. Stewart, *Bermondsey in War* (1980).

Index

Bacon, Josiah	23
Beornmund	1
Bermondsey Abbey	1-5
Bermondsey Gospel Mission	21, 22
Bermondsey Spa	9, 10
Bermondsey Settlement	25, 28
Bermondsey Square	1, 4, 10
Bermondsey Street	4, 6, 8, 9, 13
Bermondsey Wall	1, 17
Bevingtons and Sons	12, 13
The 'Blue'	27
Boutcher School	23
Braidwood, James	18
Bricklayers' Arms Station	15
Cherry Garden	9
Child, Aylwin	3
Christy and Co.	13
Courage's Brewery	19
Curtis, William	10
Donkin, Bryan	20
Galley Wall	1
Grange Road	5, 10, 13, 20, 23, 27, 29
Grange Road Baths	29
Grange Walk	4, 5, 22
Hay's Wharf	17-19
Horselydown	9
Jacob's Island	24, 25
Jamaica House	9
Jamaica Road	9, 10, 28
Keyse, Thomas	9, 10

Leather manufacture	11, 12
Lidgett, The Reverend Dr. John Scott	25
London and Greenwich Railway	14, 15
London Bridge Station	14, 15, 31
Long Lane	3, 11, 12, 20
Martin and Sons Ltd., C.W.	13
Most Holy Trinity Church	5, 21, 23
Neckinger River	1, 12
Peek, Frean and Co. Ltd.	19, 20, 29
Pope, Sir Thomas	4, 9
Public Health Centre	29
Rolls Estate	7
St. James's Church	21, 29
St. John's Church, Horselydown	22
St. Mary Magdalen's Church	1, 5-8, 22
St. Olave's Church	5, 7, 22
St. Olave's Grammar School	22
Salter, Alfred	28, 29
Sarson's Vinegar Brewery	19
Shad Thames	5, 17, 32
Spa Road Station	14, 15
Star Music Hall	27
Tanner Street	12, 24
Tanner Street Recreation Ground	5, 29, 30
Tooley Street	5, 17, 18, 22, 25, 32
Tower Bridge	15, 16
Tower Bridge Road	1, 13, 15, 22, 27
Tower Subway	15, 16
Wilson Grove	29
Workhouse, Tanner Street	24
World Wars	30